7 Day Loan

ate shown

D1448637

19

Novels for Students, Volume 35

Project Editor: Sara Constantakis Rights Acquisition and Management: Margaret Chamberlain-Gaston, Leitha Etheridge-Sims, Kelly Quin, Aja Perales Composition: Evi Abou-El-Seoud Manufacturing: Drew Kalasky

Imaging: John Watkins

Product Design: Pamela A. E. Galbreath, Jennifer Wahi Content Conversion: Katrina Coach Product Manager: Meggin Condino © 2011 Gale, Cengage Learning

Gale
27500 Drake Rd.
Farmington Hills, MI, 48331-3535

ISBN-13: 978-1-4144-6698-9
ISBN-10: 1-4144-6698-6

ISSN 1094-3552

This title is also available as an e-book.
ISBN-13: 978-1-4144-7364-2
ISBN-10: 1-4144-7364-8
Contact your Gale, a part of Cengage Learning sales
representative for ordering information.

Printed in the United States of America
1 2 3 4 5 6 7 14 13 12 11 10

Never Let Me Go

Kazuo Ishiguro
2005

Introduction

Never Let Me Go is the sixth novel by renowned British writer Kazuo Ishiguro. Published in 2005, it was short-listed for the Booker Prize. Ostensibly set in England from the 1970s to the late 1990s, *Never Let Me Go* is a futuristic, dystopian (anti-utopian) tale about human cloning. At a secluded private school in the English countryside, young people who have been created through cloning are educated. Their lives will be short, since as soon as they become adults they will be required to donate their vital organs, one by one, to those who need them to recover from disease. The novel focuses on the lives of three of these clones: Kathy, who narrates the story; Ruth; and Tommy. The author examines how they grow up, the relationships they form, and the values by which they learn to live.

Ishiguro started writing *Never Let Me Go* in 1990. In its early stages, the novel was not about cloning. Instead, the characters were doomed because they had been contaminated by some kind of nuclear material. Not satisfied with his material, Ishiguro abandoned the story twice to write *The Unconsoled* and *When We Were Orphans* before finally finishing *Never Let Me Go*. Cloning was much in the news at the time, and this supplied him with his theme.

The novel has been acclaimed for Ishiguro's subtle handling of a nightmarish theme. It has also been praised as a moving meditation on how people create meaning in life in the face of loss and mortality.

Author Biography

Ishiguro was born in Nagasaki, Japan, on November 8, 1954. The family, including Ishiguro's two sisters, moved to Britain in 1960, when Ishiguro's father, Shigeo Ishiguro, an oceanographer, was employed as a researcher at the National Institute of Oceanography. Living in Guildford, Surrey, Ishiguro attended a grammar school in Woking, Surrey. In 1973, he worked as a grouse beater (flushing out birds for hunting) for the Queen Mother at Balmoral Castle, Aberdeen, Scotland. The following year he enrolled at the University of Kent at Canterbury, graduating with degrees in English and philosophy in 1978. From 1979 to 1980, he was a residential social worker in London, assisting homeless people. Ishiguro had been writing fiction since the mid-1970s, and he enrolled in a graduate creative writing program at the University of East Anglia, where he was taught by noted writers Malcolm Bradbury and Angela Carter. He completed his master of arts degree in 1980, and in 1981, three of his short stories were published in *Introductions 7: Stories by New Writers*.

Ishiguro moved to London, and his first novel, *A Pale View of the Hills*, was published in 1982. It received excellent reviews and was awarded the Winifred Holtby Memorial Prize. Encouraged by this success, Ishiguro decided in 1982 to pursue a full-time writing career. He also became a British citizen in the same year. His second novel, *An Artist of the Floating World* (1986), won the Whitbread Book of the Year Award and was short-listed for the Booker Prize. Both of Ishiguro's first two novels featured Japanese characters, but in his third novel, Ishiguro focused entirely on a plot and setting based in his adopted country. This was *The Remains of the Day* (1989), the novel that won the Booker Prize, became an international best seller, and made him famous. Set in the 1950s, it features an elderly English butler who looks back at his thirty-five years of service to an English aristocrat and tries to justify to himself why he chose this path in life. The novel was made into a 1993 film starring Anthony Hopkins and Emma Thompson that was nominated for eight Academy Awards.

Ishiguro's fourth novel was *The Unconsoled* (1995), which is about a concert pianist in Europe who suffers odd lapses of memory and seems to live in a dreamlike environment. The novel is unlike Ishiguro's previous work; it won the Cheltenham Prize but in general received a mixed critical reception. In the same year, Ishiguro received the Order of the British Empire for services to literature. In 1998, the French government named him a Chevalier de l'Ordre des Arts et des Lettres.

In 2000, Ishiguro published his fifth novel, *When We Were Orphans*, followed in 2005 by *Never Let Me Go*. Both novels were short-listed for the Booker Prize.

As of 2009, Ishiguro lived in London with his wife, Laura Anne MacDougal, and daughter,

Naomi.

Part One

CHAPTER ONE

Never Let Me Go is set in England in the late 1990s. It is narrated by a thirty-one-year-old woman named Kathy H. At the beginning of the novel, Kathy announces that she has been a "carer" for eleven years, working with "donors." She does not explain what she means by these terms, but she does say that through being a carer she has been able to reconnect with two of her friends, Ruth and Tommy, with whom she went to school. The school was a private school in the English countryside called Hailsham. Kathy's reminiscences of the time she spent at Hailsham form a substantial part of the novel. In this chapter she recalls some incidents when she was about twelve or thirteen. Tommy was mercilessly teased by the other children. When he was not selected by the other boys to play soccer with them, he would lose his temper. The other students would make fun of him as he gave vent to his rage.

Media Adaptations

- A film adaptation (screenplay by Alex Garland) of *Never Let Me Go* will be released by DNA Films in 2010, directed by Mark Romanek and starring Keira Knightley, Sally Hawkins, Andrew Garfield, and Carey Mulligan.

CHAPTER TWO

Kathy looks back at how she took an interest in Tommy over the few weeks following the temper tantrum. There were more temper tantrums and incidents involving pranks played upon him. The children think Tommy is lazy, noting that he fails to contribute anything to the Exchange, a quarterly exhibition and sale in which students trade little items they have made themselves. Kathy relates that she has spoken to Tommy recently about his troubles at the school, and he says it started when Miss Geraldine, one of the "guardians" (the term they use instead of teacher), praised some poor painting he had done, and this aroused the resentment of the other students. Kathy resumes her reminiscence, saying that after a while the teasing of Tommy stopped. He told her it was due to something that Miss Lucy, another guardian, had said to him.

CHAPTER THREE

Tommy explains to Kathy what Miss Lucy had said to him. She said it did not matter if he was not creative, and he was not to worry about it or about what others were saying. Miss Lucy told him he was a good student. As she said this, she was shaking with rage, but Tommy did not know why she was angry. Tommy is helped by her comments, and his attitude changes, because he knows that what happens with the other students is not his fault. He also tells Kathy that Miss Lucy told him she believed the students should be told more about "donations," and Kathy seems to understand what is meant by this, but she does not explain it for the reader.

Kathy reminisces about a woman known as Madame, who comes to the school several times a year and takes the students' best artwork. The students think she puts the artwork in what they call the Gallery, but no one knows for sure what happens to it or why Madame takes it. Madame does not talk to the students, and Ruth thinks she is afraid of them. One day, a group of students surprises Madame after she has gotten out of her car, and Madame reacts with a suppressed shudder, and the students take this as confirmation that she is afraid of them. Looking back, Kathy says that even at a young age the children must have been aware at some level that they were not like other people, and that others might be afraid of them because of how they were created and what their purpose was.

CHAPTER FOUR

Kathy looks back to a time she calls the "tokens controversy," when the children were about ten. The students thought they should be compensated with tokens when Madame took something of theirs. A boy called Roy J. suggests it to Miss Emily, the head guardian, and eventually the idea is adopted. Agirl called Polly T. asks Miss Lucy why Madame takes their work in the first place, but Miss Lucy does not explain.

Kathy then reminisces about the Sales, which were where the children bought with their tokens items such as toys and clothes. The items for sale were delivered in boxes by van every month. Kathy then thinks back to the early days of her friendship with Ruth, which started when they were seven or eight and they ride imaginary horses together.

CHAPTER FIVE

Kathy reports that as adults, when she was "caring" for Ruth in Dover, they discussed how

Ruth had been the leader of the "secret guards" who protected their favorite guardian, Miss Geraldine.

Kathy became one of them. She recalls how they protected Miss Geraldine from what they were convinced was a plot to kidnap her hatched by some of the other guardians. Kathy and Ruth have a falling out, and Kathy is excluded from the secret guard fantasy, but she still remains loyal to Ruth. About three years later, Ruth implies that a pencil case she has acquired was given to her by Miss Geraldine. Guardians are not allowed to show favoritism or give gifts. Kathy knows Ruth is lying and without confronting her directly finds a way of letting Ruth know that she knows.

CHAPTER SIX

Troubled by what she has done to damage her friendship with Ruth, Kathy finds a way of making it up to her. Ruth appreciates it and looks for some way of being nice to Kathy in return. The opportunity arises over a cassette tape of songs by a popular singer, Judy Bridgewater. Before Kathy explains what happens, she digresses, commenting on how smoking was forbidden at the school. Miss Lucy tells them that she once smoked herself, but it was far worse if the children were to smoke than it ever had been for her, although she does not explain why. Going back to the tape, Kathy says that her favorite song had a line, "Baby, never let me go." She imagines that it refers to a woman who has been told she could not have babies but really wants one and has one anyway. One day, she is dancing to the music in her dorm, holding a pillow to her chest as an imaginary baby. Madame comes by the half-open door and sees her. Madame says nothing but leaves sobbing. A couple of years later, Kathy discusses the incident with Tommy; they both know by then none of the students at Hailsham are able to have children. The tape was lost a short while after the incident with Madame. Ruth takes the trouble to replace it for her with a tape of ballroom dancing music. That kind of music means nothing to Kathy, but she appreciates the gesture.

CHAPTER SEVEN

When Kathy is thirteen, Miss Lucy decides to tell them all the truth. They will not be able to do what they want to do in life. Their futures are all determined. They have been created in order that, when they become adults, they will be required to donate their vital organs for others. The children do not react much; it seems that they already know this in a vague kind of way. They have sex education classes, in which they are told they must avoid disease, but sex will be different for them than for normal people because they are unable to have babies. The children discuss the future "donations" in a lighthearted way; in fact, it becomes a sort of running joke about what awaits them. This changes when they are fifteen; they talk more seriously about it.

CHAPTER EIGHT

At age sixteen, the topic of sex often comes up among the students. They receive contradictory messages from the guardians. The guardians tell them that sex is not something to be ashamed of, but at the same time they set rules that make it difficult for the students to engage in it. Kathy thinks there is less sexual activity among the students than many of the students like to think, although she knows Ruth and Tommy have done it. She herself has held back, but she decides she wants to experiment and chooses a boy named Harry C. She starts dropping hints to him that she is interested in him, but then Ruth and Tommy split up, and this puts her in a different position.

CHAPTER NINE

After Tommy and Ruth split up, a couple of girls mention to Kathy that they expect her to become a couple with Tommy. This surprises her, but she stops trying to start something with Harry. Then Ruth asks Kathy to help her get back together with Tommy. Kathy agrees. When Kathy talks to Tommy, he tells her about something Miss Lucy has told him. She said she had been wrong to tell him earlier that it did not matter that he was not creative. The art the students produced was important, she says, partly because it is "evidence." She does not explain what she means but encourages him to work again at his art. Kathy then mentions that Ruth wants them to get back together, but Tommy seems reluctant. The next day the students learn that Miss Lucy has left Hailsham, and Tommy and Ruth get back together.

Part Two

CHAPTER TEN

Kathy recalls that after she left Hailsham, she and seven others, including Ruth and Tommy, went to the Cottages, buildings on the site of a farm that had gone out of business. They live independently for two years in rather Spartan conditions, joining a group of students who already live there and are referred to as veterans. After about two months there, Kathy and Ruth quarrel. Kathy tells Ruth about an annoying mannerism she has copied from a veteran couple, Chrissie and Rodney. Ruth does not take this well and says that Kathy is upset because Ruth has managed to make new friends. Kathy then criticizes Ruth's behavior toward Tommy.

CHAPTER ELEVEN

Kathy feels betrayed by Ruth because in their argument Ruth made an unpleasant comment about Kathy having had sex with some of the boys at the Cottages, but now, in the present, Kathy reconsiders the situation from Ruth's point of view, deciding that perhaps Ruth had some cause to be unpleasant to her. She was trying to adapt to their new life in the Cottages, and Kathy realizes that she should not judge her friend. Recollecting once more their lives at the Cottages, Kathy says that when a student left the Cottages, people rarely spoke much of them again. She remembers someone named Steve whom she never met but who kept a collection of pornographic magazines. Some of those magazines keep turning up long after Steve had left. Kathy looks at them, and Tommy finds her doing so, but she does not tell him why she is looking, nor does she herself know.

CHAPTER TWELVE

Kathy, Tommy, Ruth, Chrissie, and Rodney decide to go on a trip to Norfolk. They go because on a previous trip, Chrissie and Rodney claim to have seen someone they regard as a "possible" for Ruth. A "possible" is a person who may be the model from whom a particular clone was made. The idea that circulates among the Hailsham students is that if they can find their model, they will have a deeper idea of who they are and what their lives might become. Ruth's possible is a woman who works in an office.

CHAPTER THIRTEEN

Rodney borrows a car, and they drive to a seaside town in Norfolk. At lunch in a cafe´, they talk about a future for Ruth, working in an office, just like her possible. Ruth even thinks that Tommy will be with her. Chrissie mentions that she has heard that a couple, if they were Hailsham students, could get a "deferral." The couple must prove that they are in love, and then they would be allowed to have few years together before they are required to become donors. Kathy has heard this rumor before, circulating among the veterans at the Cottages.

CHAPTER FOURTEEN

They go shopping in the town. They pass an office with a big glass front, and Rodney points out Ruth's possible, a dark-haired woman of about fifty. Later, they see the same woman walking along the street, and they follow her into an art shop. They pretend to be interested in the pictures while observing the woman. After they leave, they decide that the woman is not a possible for Ruth after all. Chrissie and Rodney then take Ruth to visit a friend of theirs, but Kathy and Tommy decline to join them. There is tension between Ruth and Kathy.

CHAPTER FIFTEEN

Tommy and Kathy go to a shop where Kathy finds a copy of the Judy Bridgewater tape that she lost some time before. Tommy had suggested that they look for it. He had always wanted to find it for her. Later, they talk about deferrals, and Tommy wonders whether the rumor is true. He thinks it may have some connection to the Gallery, the collection of artwork that Madame took from them. The Gallery would help the authorities decide whether the couple who applied for the deferral were worthy of it. Tommy also tells Kathy he has recently been doing some art work of his own, drawing imaginary animals. Later, as they return home, Kathy feels that the tension between her and Ruth has been resolved.

CHAPTER SIXTEEN

One day Tommy shows Kathy his drawings of imaginary animals. He tells Kathy he sees no reason why he should keep his work secret, and she agrees with him. She tells him his work is good, but some time later, Kathy and Ruth talk about Tommy's animals, and they both laugh about them. When Kathy later meets Ruth and Tommy at a churchyard, Ruth is upset that Tommy told Kathy about his theory of the purpose of the Gallery but did not tell her. She then tells Tommy that Kathy thinks his drawings of animals are hilarious. Kathy is shocked that Ruth would say such a thing, and she turns and leaves.

CHAPTER SEVENTEEN

Over the next few days, Kathy realizes that Ruth and Tommy have grown apart; Kathy also finds it harder to talk to Tommy. Eventually she and Ruth try to patch up their quarrel. Ruth tells Kathy that she and Tommy probably will not be together forever, but even if they were to split up, Tommy would not be interested in taking up with Kathy. He regards her just as a friend, Ruth says. Kathy takes this without much comment, but the two girls come close to quarreling about something else and part on bad terms. Not long after that, Kathy decides to leave the Cottages and begin her training as a carer.

Part Three

CHAPTER EIGHTEEN

It is seven years since Kathy left the Cottages, and she reports on her life as a carer, saying she is suited to it. She drives around the country, taking care of the donors that are assigned to her. She has learned to live with the emotional difficulties of the work and the long hours. One day she meets Laura, one of her friends from Hailsham, by chance, and Laura says she has heard that Ruth had a bad first donation. Laura suggests that Kathy become Ruth's carer. They also discuss the fact that Hailsham has been closed. Three weeks later, Kathy does become Ruth's carer. Their relationship is still a little strained, and Kathy feels that Ruth does not trust her. They decide to go to see an old boat that is stranded in the marshes.

CHAPTER NINETEEN

On the way to see the boat, they stop at Kings field, which is a recovery center for donors. Tommy is staying there, and the three of them drive to see the boat. They talk about the news that Chrissie has "completed" (that is, died) during her second donation. On the way home Ruth asks Kathy to forgive her for trying, at Hailsham and the Cottages, to keep Kathy and Tommy apart. She wants Kathy to put it right by applying for a deferral, so she can spend some years with Tommy. She gives them Madame's address, which she discovered for herself. After this, Kathy's relationship with Ruth improves, and just before Ruth dies after her second donation, Kathy agrees to become Tommy's carer.

CHAPTER TWENTY

A year later, Kathy becomes Tommy's carer.

He has just made his third donation. Their relationship deepens, but Kathy regrets that they left it so late. Tommy continues to do his drawings of imaginary animals. Some time later, Kathy tells Tommy that she has seen Madame after waiting outside her house in Little hampton. They decide to visit her and ask for a deferral. Tommy says he will take his drawings.

CHAPTER TWENTY-ONE

Kathy and Tommy intercept Madame as she is about to go into her house. They say they must speak with her, and she invites them in. Kathy explains that she and Tommy are in love and want to apply for a deferral. Tommy explains his belief about the purpose of Madame's gallery, that the students' art will reveal who they are. Then someone in a wheelchair enters the room, and Tommy and Kathy realize it is Miss Emily, the former head guardian at Hailsham.

CHAPTER TWENTY-TWO

Miss Emily remembers both of them. She tells them the rumor about deferrals is untrue; there is no such thing. She also says that their artwork was taken to prove to doubters that these cloned people had souls, just like normal people. She explains that Hailsham was set up to improve the conditions under which clones lived, which had been deplorable. Those who set up Hailsham wanted to show that clones could become fully human if given a decent education but at some point there was a scandal involving a researcher who claimed to be able to help people produce superior children through genetic manipulation. People found this alarming, and funding for Hailsham began to dry up, even though Hailsham had nothing to do with the researcher's work. Miss Emily also explains that Miss Lucy was dismissed as a guardian because she thought the students should be told more of who they were and what their lives were for. Miss Emily believes Miss Lucy was wrong and that it was important to shelter the children from the full truth. When Kathy and Tommy drive home, Tommy says he agrees with Miss Lucy. He gets out of the car and gives vent to his feelings.

CHAPTER TWENTY-THREE

Tommy starts to identify more with the other donors at the center where he lives, and Kathy feels a bit left out. Tommy sometimes tells her she cannot understand certain things because she is not a donor. Tommy's fourth donation is coming up, and he tells Kathy he thinks he ought to have another carer because the job is too much for Kathy. She is angry at first but then agrees to his suggestion. In the last section of the book, Kathy looks back from the present. She is still a carer. Tommy is dead, but she thinks she will never forget her memories of him and Ruth.

Characters

Chrissie

Chrissie is one of the veterans at the Cottages. Chrissie is very welcoming to Kathy when she and the others first arrive from Hailsham, and everything about Hailsham fascinates her. She is always asking questions about it. Chrissie's boyfriend is Rodney, and they are always seen together. Chrissie is the dominant partner, and Rodney defers to her opinions. Chrissie becomes a donor and dies during her second donation.

Cynthia E.

Cynthia E. is a student at Hailsham and one of Kathy's friends. It is she who says she expects Kathy to take up with Tommy when Tommy and Ruth split up.

Miss Emily

Miss Emily is the head guardian at Hailsham. She is older than the other guardians, and the students are intimidated by her but they also regard her as fair-minded and do not argue with her decisions. At morning assemblies, she often tells the students they are special and should use the opportunities they are given. At the end of the novel, Kathy and Tommy meet Miss Emily again at Madame's house. She is in a wheelchair, and she explains to them how Hailsham was an attempt to give the students better lives than they would otherwise, as clones, have been able to lead. She believes that in her work at Hailsham she was able to give them their childhoods, even if that meant keeping them in the dark on some important matters.

Miss Geraldine

Miss Geraldine is one of the guardians at Hailsham. She is the favorite of the students, since she is always gentle and kind. She even finds something to praise in Tommy's bad drawing of an elephant.

Hannah

Hannah is a student at Hailsham. She and Kathy have been friends since they were five or six years old. She is also close friends with Ruth, but she does not play a large role in the story.

Harry C.

Harry C. is a student at Hailsham. He is respectable and quiet, and Kathy at one point wants to form a sexual relationship with him, but this never actually happens. Other than that, he and Kathy do not have much to do with each other, and Harry does not go to the Cottages. Many years later,

Kathy sees him after he has made a donation.

Kathy H.

Kathy H. is the narrator of the novel. She is thirty one years old and is looking back at her life and relationships. As a child, she is a student at Hailsham. Her best friend is Ruth, and she is also friends with Tommy. Later, she lives at the Cottages and then becomes a carer at the age of twenty.

Kathy gives the impression of being a calm, reflective, level-headed woman. She is not a leader, but she fits in well with others. Like the other characters, she does not protest against the course her life must take but accepts it. This does not mean, however, that she does not occasionally have a desire for some other kind of life. She is deeply moved by a popular song that contains the line "Baby, never let me go," and she imagines it being sung by a woman who has been told she cannot have children but who has a baby nonetheless. The fact that Kathy is so moved by this song suggests that deep down, she wants to have children of her own, which she will never be able to do. Also, when Kathy is in love with Tommy, she seeks a deferral so she will be able to enjoy their relationship for longer, although when she finds that is not possible she is not devastated by the news.

Kathy's job as a carer suits her. She travels from place to place, looking after those who are donating their organs. She becomes Ruth's carer and then Tommy's. Kathy values her relationships, especially those with Ruth and Tommy, and she spends much time cultivating them. She is a sensitive woman, able to appreciate the feelings of others and take them into account. She is continually reflecting on her experiences and what they mean to her. In particular, she cannot forget Hailsham, the private school where she and the others were educated. She knows that it was a special place, and she believes that she, Ruth, and Tommy were very fortunate to be able to go there. At the end of the novel, she has eight more months to serve as a carer, after which she will become a donor.

Keffers

Keffers is a gruff, uncommunicative man who oversees the maintenance of the Cottages.

Laura

Laura is a student at Hailsham and one of Kathy's friends. She is the joker in the group, always ready with an amusing remark. When they are all about thirteen she enthusiastically takes part in the mocking of Tommy. However, Laura does not fare well as a carer, frustrated by the demands of the job. When Kathy meets her after a gap of seven years, Laura has lost the lively spark she used to have.

Miss Lucy

Miss Lucy is one of the guardians at Hailsham. Her full name is Lucy Wainright. Miss Lucy excels at sports and is very strong and fit. Kathy realizes during her last years at Hailsham that Miss Lucy is different from the other guardians, although she does not really know why. Miss Lucy appears worried or frustrated by something. Then one day Miss Lucy addresses the students outside the sports pavilion. She has heard one of the students talking about possibly becoming an actor, and she tells them exactly what is in store for them. Their lives are predetermined. They should know who they are and what their lives are for. Not long after this, Miss Lucy leaves Hailsham, but the students do not know why. Many years later, Miss Emily explains to Kathy and Tommy that Miss Lucy was dismissed from her position. Miss Emily disagreed with her belief that the students should be told more about their lives. Miss Emily thinks Miss Lucy was too idealistic and did not have a good understanding of the practicalities of the situation.

Madame

Madame is presented at first as a mysterious woman who visits Hailsham several times a year and takes some of the students' artwork. The students think she must exhibit the art somewhere in what they call the Gallery. They call her Madame because she is French or Belgian. She is a tall woman who wears a gray suit, and the students think she is afraid of them—for some reason they do not understand. Many years later, Kathy and

Tommy go to visit Madame at her house in Littlehampton. They learn that Madame, along with Miss Emily, was one of the main organizers of the Hailsham project. Miss Emily tells them that Madame, to whom she refers as Marie-Claude, worked hard to make the Hailsham project succeed but has been disillusioned about how things actually turned out.

Moira B.

Moira B. is one of Kathy's friends at Hailsham. Like Kathy, she is a member of the "secret guard" fantasy regarding Miss Geraldine, and also like Kathy, she is expelled from the group.

Patricia C.

Patricia C. is a student at Hailsham and is two years younger than Kathy. She has artistic talent, and Kathy acquires her beautiful calendar at one of the Exchanges.

Peter J.

Peter J. is a student at Hailsham. It is his comment about possibly becoming an actor that prompts Miss Lucy to explain to the students what their lives will really be like.

Polly T.

Polly T. is a student at Hailsham. It is Polly

who asks Miss Lucy the question about why Madame takes their artwork.

Rodney

Rodney is living at the Cottages when Kathy first meets him. His girlfriend is Chrissie. Rodney wears his hair in a ponytail and is interested in religious concepts such as reincarnation. On a trip to Norfolk with Chrissie, Rodney spots Ruth's possible, and this prompts Ruth, Kathy, and Tommy to accompany them on another Norfolk expedition to find out if there is any truth in the sighting.

Roger C.

Roger C. is a former student at Hailsham. He was a year below Kathy. Kathy runs into him much later, at a clinic, and he tells her that Hailsham is about to close.

Roy J.

Roy J. is a year above Kathy at Hailsham. He goes to see Miss Emily to ask whether the students could receive tokens when their artwork is taken by Madame.

Ruth

Ruth is a student at Hailsham. She is close friends with Kathy from the age of seven or eight. Ruth is a leader of their small group of girls, and she can be outspoken, angry, and even vindictive sometimes. When she becomes a teenager, she and Tommy become a couple. Kathy and Ruth have a rather difficult relationship at Hailsham. In one sense, Kathy feels she is able to trust Ruth and confide in her, but Ruth can be quarrelsome, and from time to time they fall out. However, Kathy still remains loyal to Ruth, and the two girls find ways of making up to each other. When they are together at the Cottages, the girls quarrel again when Ruth makes some unpleasant, catty remarks to Kathy. Kathy is also annoyed with Ruth because Ruth is always trying to impress the veterans—the other young people at the Cottages who did not attend Hailsham, and Ruth will sometimes ignore Kathy and Tommy. Acting out of jealousy, Ruth also tries her best to keep Tommy and Kathy apart. Much later, however, after Ruth has become a donor, she asks Kathy, who is her carer, to forgive her for her bad behavior. To make up for it, Ruth suggests that Kathy and Tommy seek a deferral, so they can spend some years together. This gesture of friendship and atonement results in an improvement in the relationship between Kathy and Ruth. Ruth, however, dies after her second donation. Kathy remembers her with affection.

Steve

Steve is a former resident of the Cottages. He does not actually appear in the narrative, but he is known for his collection of pornographic magazines, which keep turning up even though he is no longer there.

Tommy

Tommy is a student at Hailsham. When he is a young boy, Tommy is subject to temper tantrums at the school. As a result of this, he is teased relentlessly by the other children but this phase passes, and Tommy emerges as an intelligent, thoughtful boy. He is good at sports but appears to have little talent for art. Tommy forms a romantic relationship with Ruth, and he is also friends with Kathy. When Tommy and Ruth split up, it seems as if he and Kathy will get together, but Tommy and Ruth soon resume their relationship. After Hailsham, Tommy lives in the Cottages with the other students from Hailsham. His relationship with Kathy deepens, although for a long time they acknowledge each other only as friends rather than romantic partners. Tommy confides in Kathy more than he does in Ruth. He tells her, for example, that he has started doing some artwork, remembering that Miss Lucy at Hailsham had told him it was important (after she had initially told him it was not). Tommy draws small imaginary animals. Even though Ruth acknowledges that she and Tommy are growing apart, she still does her best to ensure that Tommy and Kathy do not get close, either. Some years later, however, at Ruth's suggestion, Kathy becomes Tommy's carer. He has started his organ donations. Their relationship then flourishes as it had not been allowed to before. Tommy shows himself to be a mature, goodhearted individual, capable of loving Kathy. He and Kathy visit Madame so they can tell her they are in love and ask for a deferral of the time when they will have to donate their organs. They learn there is no such thing as a deferral. When Tommy's fourth donation looms, he tells Kathy he wants another carer, so that Kathy can be spared the strain of looking after him. Kathy reluctantly agrees to his request. After Tommy dies, Kathy, looking back on events, knows that she will never forget him.

Cloning

Although this is in a sense a science fiction story in that the author presents a society in which the cloning of human beings is an accepted practice, he seems to have no interest in describing the kind of society that has permitted this practice to occur or how it developed. He does make it clear, though, that in this imagined society, life for most clones is not good. When the practice first began in the early 1950s, clones were raised in extremely inhumane conditions; people believed that the clones were not fully human and did not possess a soul. They existed solely for medical purposes and were required to donate their organs so that others might recover from previously fatal diseases, such as cancer. The private school Hailsham was established to counter that view, to allow the clones to have an education, and to show that they were capable of artistic endeavors that revealed their depth of character, if not their soul. In the 1990s, after the Hailsham experiment runs out of funds, the clones are raised in large government homes. These homes, according to Miss Emily, are slightly better than they were before Hailsham, but she also tells Kathy and Tommy "you'd not sleep for days if you saw what still goes on in some of those places." The novel might therefore be read as a warning against where the biomedical sciences may be heading and the moral issues it raises. In the society depicted in the novel, the desire for scientific progress and the curing of diseases is so great that a proper examination of the moral implications of cloning has not been done, and the result is that thousands of clones are condemned to live short, circumscribed lives, regarded by most as sufficiently human in a physical sense to donate organs to the sick but not human enough to be given any basic human rights.

Topics for Further Study

- In a small group of students, discuss the ethical issues associated with cloning, especially the cloning of humans. Should this be banned by law, or should scientists be allowed to explore the possibilities? If you argue for the cloning of humans to be banned, make sure you explain your reasoning. Is your objection moral or religious or practical (that is, cloning of humans could not be done safely)? When the group finishes the discussion, each member should write a position paper that summarizes their own views on the subject.

- Watch the movie *Blade Runner* (1982). One of the issues addressed in the film is cloning. How does the treatment of cloning in this film differ from how it is presented in *Never Let Me Go* ? Write a short essay in which you present your findings.

- Read *Taylor Five* (2002), a novel for young adults by Ann Halam. Taylor is a fourteen-year-old clone living in Borneo, an island in Southeast Asia. She is one of the first human clones and resents it. During the course of this adventure story, she struggles to understand exactly who she is and what her life is all about. In an essay, discuss the similarities and differences between how Taylor learns to understands herself and how the clones in *Never Let Me Go* think of themselves and their own lives.

- Using your library and the Internet,

create a time line for the history of cloning from the second half of the twentieth century to the present. What are the major landmarks in this developing science? What laws have been passed to deal with cloning in the United States and around the world? Create a presentation in PowerPoint or similar software and show it to your class.

Relationships

The clones in the novel all have short lives, and they know it. It seems that they live only into their twenties or thirties. In these truncated lives, with a sure and known end, they do their best to create meaning. They come to know what is important in life, and it is not longevity. Far more important than a long life is a rich, satisfying one with warm and positive human relationships. Kathy and her friends Ruth and Tommy may be flawed as people, as all humans are, but they learn how to care for one another, how to overcome past slights or disappointments. They learn how to talk to one another, to communicate what is important to them. As they emerge from childhood into adulthood, they have plenty of time to reflect on their mortality, and they also accept their role in life. They do not protest about it or try to alter it. They are not angry about it. They accept their fates. On a few occasions they do entertain ideas about what they might do with their lives that turn out to be unrealistic—Ruth thinks she may work in an office one day, for example—but when the truth dawns it does so gently, without sparking great dismay. Even when Tommy and Kathy fall in love and seek a deferral so that they may have more time to enjoy their relationship, they are not seeking to escape altogether from their prescribed lives, only to postpone their donations for a little while. Through the lens of a highly imaginative story, the author has created in effect a universal meditation, through his doomed characters, on what makes life worth living in the face of the unalterable fact of human mortality.

Deception

At Hailsham, the children are not told much about what others have decided is their sole purpose in life. It is not that they are told nothing, but as Kathy remarks, looking back on the matter as an adult, it seems that they were given information that was always a little too advanced for them to understand. Either that or the truth was explained to them in away that ensured they would not really be aware of its full import. An example of this is when they are told about sex at the age of about thirteen. Kathy thinks that when the guardians gave lectures about sex, they also explained about donations, but because the children were mostly curious about sex they forgot or did not notice the information about donations. This was probably, Kathy thinks, deliberate on the part of the guardians. The children were, as she puts it, "told and not told." They were also told about how important sex is because it can involve the emotions; therefore they should be careful and treat it as special, like everyone else did. This was in spite of the fact that they were not able to have babies. In other words, the information about not being able to have babies was slipped in along with a talk that still emphasized the importance of sex.

One day Miss Lucy does try to explain to the children what awaits them, but later Kathy is not sure how much Miss Lucy actually said. Kathy guesses that "once she'd seen the puzzled, uncomfortable faces in front of her, she realised the impossibility of completing what she'd started." Furthermore, Kathy recalls that after the talk, the students discussed Miss Lucy herself rather than what she said; some students thought she had gone crazy; others thought she had merely been scolding them for being too noisy.

When Tommy and Kathy later visit Madame and find Miss Emily there, Miss Emily explains the dispute she had with Miss Lucy. Miss Lucy was in favor of complete disclosure to the students about the real nature of their lives and their future, but Miss Emily wanted the children to be shielded from the full truth. She thought she was helping them by doing so; the deception, in her view, was necessary. Otherwise the children could not have been happy. She admits that "sometimes … we kept things from you, lied to you. Yes, in many ways we *fooled* you…. But we sheltered you … and we gave you your childhoods."

The theme of necessary deception suggests in a wider sense the fact that children are often shielded by their parents about truths they are too young to understand. How much to tell a child, and when, is a judgment every parent must make, but in the novel, as Kathy and Tommy leave after their conversation with Miss Emily, Tommy expresses his belief that Miss Lucy was right—the students should have been told more about the future that awaited them.

Style

Dystopia

The novel can be described by the term dystopia. In dystopian fiction, the author takes a problematic aspect of contemporary society and projects it onto a larger scale, imagining a bleak and depressing future for humankind. Examples of dystopian novels include Aldous Huxley's *Brave New World* (1932), which features a society in which cloning takes place; George Orwell's *1984* (1949); and Margaret Atwood's *The Handmaid's Tale* (1985). Dystopian fiction is the opposite of utopian fiction, which describes an ideal way of life.

Euphemism

A euphemism is a term that softens the impact of something that is disturbing or offensive by making it sound vague or neutral. Dystopias often include the manipulation of language by those in power to blur the impact of oppressive policies. In Atwood's *The Handmaid's Tale*, for example, a deformed baby is referred to as an "unbaby," which defines it in a way that makes it easier for the authorities to kill such babies. In *Never Let Me Go*, the clones refer to death as "completing." They never use the terms die, dying, or death. For example, Ruth says to Kathy, "I heard about Chrissie. I heard she completed during her second donation." "Completing" has none of the emotional impact of the word death. It does, however, express the idea that the clones have finished what they were created to do. They have completed their life purpose. The term therefore has for them a positive connotation, which may explain how they are able to face their inevitable fate with such tranquility.

Narrative Flashback

The story starts in the late 1990s, when Kathy is thirty-one years old. It is then told in the form of Kathy's memories of her life, starting when she was a young girl at Hailsham. This structure is maintained throughout the first two parts of the novel. Kathy reflects, from the standpoint of adulthood, on her childhood and adolescence. These reminiscences might be called flashbacks—a flashback is a scene that takes place before the main time frame of the novel—but since they form the bulk of the narrative they are rather too long for that term to be appropriate. The author's technique of telling the story is to provide long stretches of narrative in which Kathy recalls her childhood but occasionally (the beginning of chapter four, the second section of chapter six, the beginning of chapter ten, and elsewhere) return to Kathy's life in the present as she drives around the country fulfilling her duties as a carer. The structure changes in part three, in which Kathy tells of the more recent past, from her present perspective as a carer.

Cloning in the 1990s

Lee M. Silver, in *Remaking Eden: Cloning and Beyond in a Brave New World*, defines cloning as "the process by which a cell, or group of cells, from one individual organism is used to derive an entirely new organism." The new organism is genetically identical to that from which it is derived.

In 1996, there was a major breakthrough in reproductive technology when a British scientist, Ian Wilmut, working with colleagues at the Roslin Institute near Edinburgh, Scotland, successfully created a healthy lamb called Dolly from a single cell taken from an adult ewe. Dolly was in essence an identical twin of the ewe. This remarkable breakthrough was announced in the journal *Nature* on February 27, 1997.

According to Wilmut, one of the purposes of cloning sheep and eventually other animals was to transplant their organs into humans to cure disease. Quoted in Susan Squier's essay, "Negotiating Boundaries: From Assisted Reproduction to Assisted Replication," Wilmut said, "There are about 160,000 people a year who die before organs like hearts, livers, and kidneys become available to them." He added that cloning would be an effective way of providing organs that could be used to treat such conditions. At the time in Britain, however, there was a debate about the ethical issues that might be involved in transplanting the organs of animals into humans. Would humans be affected by this in some fundamental way?Would it blur the distinction between humans and animals?

The creation of Dolly in 1996 shows that in *Never Let Me Go*, which on the face of it seems a fantastic story, Ishiguro was merely drawing on current scientific research and controversy, merely substituting cloned humans for cloned sheep and other animals.

The announcement about the cloning of Dolly produced an avalanche of publicity and media speculation about cloning as it might be developed and applied to humans. Some scientists argued that the technology involved in cloning animals might not necessarily work to clone humans, that such a possibility was unlikely in the foreseeable future, and that there would be no reason to do it anyway. Other scientists believed that such technology could be applied safely to human cloning, without risk of birth defects.

Opposition to Human Cloning

Because of the serious ethical issues it raised, human cloning was already banned in Britain in the 1990s, and public opinion was firmly against it. In the United States, a Time/CNN poll appearing in *Time* magazine a few weeks after the announcement of the cloning of Dolly showed that 74 percent of respondents thought that it was against God's will to clone human beings. Another poll showed that two-thirds of Americans also thought that the cloning of animals was wrong.

Silver brought attention to the widespread fear of cloning that existed, and may still exist, among the general public. He argued that the fear was due to misperceptions among the public about what cloning is. It does not mean that a cloned human would be exactly the same as its original in terms of consciousness, personality, feelings, and other attributes. Silver explains as follows:

> Real biological cloning can only take place at the level of the cell—life *in the general sense*. It is only long after the cloning event is completed that a unique—and independent—life *in the special sense* could emerge in the developing fetus.

Ishiguro alludes to this question in the novel. The clones at Hailsham believe that if they could locate the person from whom they were created, they would have "*some* insight into who you were deep down, and maybe too you'd see something of what your life held in store." In other words, they believe there will be some similarities between themselves and the person from whom they were "copied" (as they put it), but they will not be identical in every way to them.

The second misperception, according to Silver, was that clones would be an "imperfect imitation of the real thing. This causes some people to think that

—far from having the same soul as someone else—a clone would have no soul at all." This idea finds its way directly into *Never Let Me Go*. The general population in the society depicted believes that the clones do not possess a soul. The school Hailsham was set up to counter this predominant view, and it is why the students there are encouraged to pursue art to reveal the depths of their inner life. Silver argues that such a debate about whether clones would have souls is based on a misunderstanding. He points out, "The newly created embryo can only develop inside the womb of a woman in the same way that all embryos and fetuses develop. Cloned children will be full-fledged human beings."

Critical Overview

Never Let Me Go received universal praise from reviewers, many of whom regarded the novel as Ishiguro's best since *The Remains of the Day*. A reviewer for *Publishers Weekly* admires Ishiguro's style, commenting that the novel is "so exquisitely observed that even the most workaday objects and interactions are infused with a luminous, humming otherworldliness." The reviewer concludes that the novel is "a stinging cautionary tale of science outpacing ethics." For Joseph O'Neill in the *Atlantic*, the novel is "the saddest, most persuasive science fiction you'll read." O'Neill points out that Ishiguro brings attention to the fact that "modern desperation regarding death, combined with technological advances and the natural human capacity for self-serving fictions and evasions … could easily give rise to new varieties of socially approved atrocities." In *National Review*, Gina R. Dalfonzo calls the novel a "quietly devastating, beautifully written tale…. Ishiguro ensures that, having known Kathy's world, we will look at our own through changed eyes." Stephen Bernstein, in the *Review of Contemporary Fiction*, notes that Ishiguro's stylistic technique in *Never Let Me Go* is similar to that which he has employed in many of his previous novels. He describes it as "Ishiguro's penchant for the slow revelation of a first-person narrator's inner secrets." Bernstein concludes that the novel is a "powerful and sad narrative…. One whose lingering implications we will do well to take to heart." Finally, Sarah Howard, in *Kliatt*, recommends the novel for high school seniors. She writes: "Melancholy, suspenseful, and at times alarming, this novel is a compellingly dark pageturner."

Sources

Bernstein, Stephen, Review of *Never Let Me Go*, in *Review of Contemporary Fiction*, Vol. 25, No. 1, Spring 2005, p. 139.

Dalfonzo, Gina R., "Lucky Pawns," in *National Review*, Vol. 57, No. 1, June 20, 2005, p. 53.

Howard, Sarah, Review of *Never Let Me Go*, in *Kliatt*, Vol. 40, No. 5, September 2006, p. 24.

Ishiguro, Kazuo, *Never Let Me Go*, Vintage Books, 2005.

Kluger, Jeffrey, "Will We Follow the Sheep?," in *Time*, Vol. 109, No. 10, March 10, 1997, p. 71.

O'Neill, Joseph, Review of *Never Let Me Go*, in *Atlantic*, Vol. 295, No. 4, May 2005, p. 123.

Review of *Never Let Me Go*, in *Publishers Weekly*, Vol. 252, No. 5, January 31, 2005, p. 46.

Silver, Lee M., *Remaking Eden: Cloning and Beyond in a Brave New World*, Avon Books, 1997, pp. 9–10, 93–94.

Squier, Susan, "Negotiating Boundaries: From Assisted Reproduction to Assisted Replication," in *Playing Dolly: Technocultural Formations, Fantasies, & Fictions*, edited by E. Ann Kaplan and Susan Squier, Rutgers University Press, 1999, p. 111.

Wong, Cynthia F., and Grace Crummett, "A

Conversation about Life and Art with Kazuo Ishiguro," in *Conversations with Kazuo Ishiguro*, edited by Brian W. Schaffer and Cynthia F. Wong, University Press of Mississippi, 2008, pp. 214, 215, 219.

Further Reading

Levine, Aaron D., *Cloning: A Beginner's Guide*, One world Publications, 2007.

> This is an explanation for beginners to the complex, developing science of cloning. Levine discusses, among many other topics, the ethical issues surrounding the idea of cloning humans.

Schaffer, Brian W., *Understanding Kazuo Ishiguro*, University of South Carolina Press, 2008.

> This is a guide to Ishiguro's work for students and general readers. Schaffer shows Ishiguro's debt to Japanese literature and writers such as Joseph Conrad, E. M. Forster, and James Joyce, as well as to Freudian psychoanalysis.

Sim, Wai-chew, *Kazuo Ishiguro: A Routledge Guide*, Routledge, 2009.

> This book contains a biographical survey and an introduction to all of Ishiguro's work, including an overview of different interpretations. There are also sections on issues connected to Ishiguro's work, such as postcolonial studies and narrative theory.

Wong, Cynthia F., *Kazuo Ishiguro*, Northcote House, 2000.

> This is a concise guide to Ishiguro's work and contains analyses of his first four novels, up to *The Unconsoled*. Wong emphasizes the role played by memory in these works.

Suggested Search Terms

Kazuo Ishiguro

Never Let Me Go

Never Let Me Go AND cloning

Kazuo Ishiguro AND dystopia

Kazuo Ishiguro AND cloning

Dolly AND cloning AND sheep

Kazuo Ishiguro AND Never Let Me Go

Never Let Me Go AND song

11 DEC 2023 S